WHY I CAME TO JUDEVINE

Other works by David Budbill

Poetry
From Down to the Village
The Chain Saw Dance
The Barking Dog

Plays
Judevine
Pulp Cutters' Nativity
Knucklehead Rides Again
Mannequins' Demise

Novels
Bones on Black Spruce Mountain

Short Stories
Snowshoe Trek to Otter River

Children's Books
Christmas Tree Farm

WHY I CAME TO JUDEVINE

David Budbill

Drawings by Lois Eby

WHITE PINE PRESS

Grateful acknowledgement to the following magazines in which some of these poems first appeared: *Beloit Poetry Journal, Longhouse, New Letters,* and *White Pine Journal.*

"Why I Came to Judevine" originally appeared under the title "Man at the Breech: My Uncle Freddy" in *The Ohio Review.* Spring/Summer 1978.

"North" is an excerpt from and a revision of "Journey for the North" which first appeared in my book of poems *From Down to the Village* (The Ark, 35 Highland Avenue, Cambridge, MA 02139), 1981.

"Tommy Stames" first appeared in my book of poems *The Chain Saw Dance* (Countryman Press, Woodstock, VT 05091), 1977.

"Gossip at the Rink" is a scene from my play *Judevine.* It grew out of a series of improvisations during rehersals for two of the productions of the play, and it therefore has, in a way, more than one author. I would like here to acknowledge the actors who helped me write this particular piece. My grateful thanks to: Kelly Andrews, Tom Blachly, Deborah Bremer, Thomas Butler, Rusty DeWees, Deborah Freeman, and Patti Quinn.

The quotation from Sophocles is taken from the Fitts/Fitzgerald translation of *Antigone.*

This publication was made possible, in part, by a grant from the New York State Council on the Arts.

ISBN 0-934834-14-8

Published by White Pine Press
            76 Center Street
            Fredonia, New York 14063

CONTENTS

Numberless are the world's wonders,
And none more wonderful than man.
                                    —Sophocles

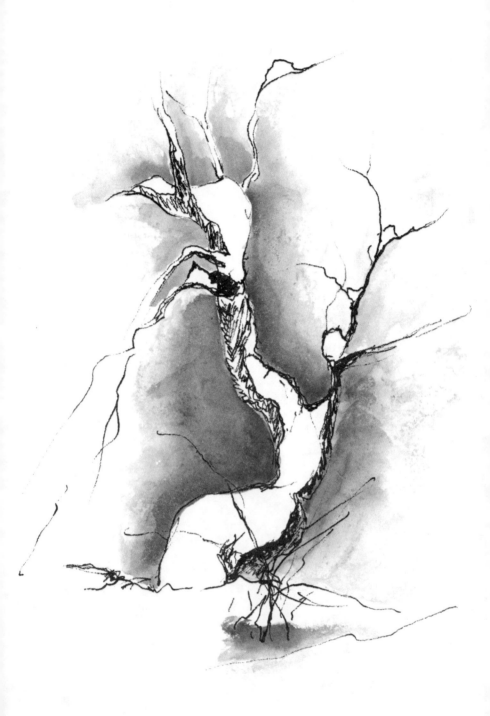

WHY I CAME TO JUDEVINE

Cleveland. 1953. Gertrude and Freddy, my aunt and uncle, live on the east side, Alhambra Street, an Italian neighborhood. Freddy's last name was Modine. He ran a metal lathe at Picker X-ray. A good job; he didn't have to go outside and therefore had work in any weather, and he didn't have to lift or bend, and the union scale was good or better than anything he had ever known before.

Alhambra Street was trying hard in 1953 to raise itself above its past. Everyone washed and waxed his car at least once a week, kept a postage stamp lawn of creeping bent, smoother, greener, more dense than any golf green in existence. And Alhambra Street was trying hard to do away with street life. Standing and drinking in the open was not a part of its vision of the future. People stayed inside, to themselves, watched their new TVs, just like the people in the suburbs. Going there may have been impossible, but acting like it was not.

But on summer evenings the old ways came back. Maybe it was just the city heat, no breeze, or maybe it was remorse for such total abjuration of the past. Whatever it was, it drew them out onto the porches. Two porches to every house, one up, one down, what we called a "double house"—a house on top of a house. Because of the climb the upper house was rented cheaper, but on summer nights, when the porches filled, it was the better place to be. You could lean on the railing and command the street.

On those summer evenings the men came home from the factories in their shiny Fords and Chevies, squeezed them into narrow drives between the houses, climbed the stairs, drank their beer, ate their garlic and sausages, and then left the television dark and went onto the porches.

They sat on gliders, smoked and rocked; or put themselves backward into straight-backed chairs, folded their arms over the top, and stared blankly into the street. Then, slowly, the shouting from porch to porch, back and forth, began, about how if that nigger Larry Doby struck out one more time they'd kill the bastard. And in their hearts they were angry, jealous, and resentful that a black man, so handsome, smooth, and famous, could be the subject of their voices.

Then the women, the fat women, having done the dishes, also came onto the porches and sat on the gliders and also rocked, their hands folded gently across their abdomens, laid gently like little balls of dough on their damp aprons. Or they stood, the outside heel of each wrist propped on their hips, fingers dangling.

After the women settled themselves, the men would rise, as if unnerved by the presence of their wives, lean over the railing and stare, or pace a bit across the porch in their white socks, their ubiquitous undershirts—not t-shirts, those were for another class, another age, but undershirts—sleeveless, white and ribbed, and the beer bellies drooping.

They were factory workers, all of them, every one, employees of American Steel, Republic Steel, Jones and Laughlin, Hanna Paints, Glidden Paints, Addressograph-Multigraph, Van Dorn Iron, U.S. Aluminum, Picker X-ray, Allied Chemical, Apex Motors, White Motors, Cleveland Hardware, Clark Controller, Cleveland Welding, Ferro Manufacturing, Eberhard Manufacturing, Eton Manufacturing, Chase Brass, Cleveland Graphite, Vulcan Tool and Die, Tinnerman Speednut, American Spool and Wire; house after double house, street after street, Italians, Lithuanians, Slavs, Poles, Hungarians, Slovacks, neighborhood pressed against neighborhood, and union men every one, United Steel Workers of America, United Chemical Workers of America, United Sheet Metal Workers of America, UAW, UEW, AFL-CIO, every one.

When it began to darken and they felt the cooling air on their naked arms, the people went inside and turned on their televisions. But when my Uncle Freddy left the porch, he passed through the living room into the kitchen where, maybe, he took down from the cupboard a new pack of Camels, then moved slowly, almost shuffling, to the hallway, the bathroom in front of him, the bedroom to his right, and to his left, the spare bedroom, his den.

Maybe he paused there in the hallway for a moment, slowly opened the new pack of cigarets, slowly lit one, wheezed his emphysemic wheeze a time or two, and waited to smell the heavy tobacco smoke mix with the smells of supper's tomato sauce and pasta. Then he turned toward the door of his den and closed himself inside that room for the evening.

I was only in his den a couple of times; once would have been enough. Twenty-three years later that place is as vivid to me as the mountains are outside my window at this moment.

Stand in the doorway. Step in. Turn right and face the outside wall. There is one window in the middle with a dark green shade, the kind for keeping out all light, no doubt left over from the blackouts during the war. The shade is always drawn. Old and dirty, green and silver wallpaper is on the wall, as on all the walls in this room. To the right of the window, a calendar with a photograph of a mostly naked woman. Her lips are pursed. She stares outward, a catatonic stare, the kind Kim Novak stared at William Holden from the swing in the park in the motion picture "Picnic."

Turn left and face another wall. There is a day-bed up against this one; it is also green but darker. Next to it, to the left, is a little wooden keg, and on top of it is a stack of worn copies of *Saga* and *Field and Stream*. Uncle Freddy never read anything but *Saga* and *Field and Stream*; he never read the newspaper.

Tacked to the wall above the couch is a fake leopard skin, cut from some car upholstery, and hooked to it, dangling treacherously, are a dozen fishing lures: musky baits, big ones, some of them a foot long, looking ludicrous and mean. They hang there waiting for water, action, a monstrous fish gored through the mouth, thrashing and boiling the lake behind the boat, a man, my Uncle Freddy, at the other end of the line, his teeth clenched in battle, his lips slightly smiling, his blood banging against his temples. And above the leopard skin and baits, also fastened to the wall, are two fishing rods and reels, crossed like swords.

Turn left again and face another wall. High up in the right hand corner, where the ceiling and the walls converge, a minnow seine drapes gracefully halfway to the center of the ceiling, filling the corner and sagging almost halfway to the floor. The soft curves of the brown netting make a hammock, and in the hammock a few pieces of water-worn cork and a piece of gray, featherlight driftwood rest gently, in a stillness they must have known once on a summer evening, the sun going down, water lapping against the shore.

In the center of this wall stands Uncle Freddy's gun cabinet. Once, maybe twice, Uncle Freddy had unlocked the glass door and let me hold the guns. There was a .218 Bee with an 8 power Weaver scope for killing woodchucks, and a big 12 gauge Ithaca with a 30 inch barrel and full choke for ducks and geese, and a Winchester 94, a 30-30, for deer. But the object of my desire, the only one I cared about, was the 16 gauge, double-barrel, side by side, Fox. The stock and forearm were delicately checkered, and the dark walnut glistened with a deep patina from years of Freddy's oil and rubbing. At the breech, engraved in the metal, was a tiny hunting scene of a man and a dog at point and a partridge exploding away and trees and grass, and all that in a space no more than two inches long by one inch high. It was a vision of our dream.

I always hoped when Freddy died I'd get that 16 gauge but I didn't. I didn't even get it after Aunt Gertrude died.

All the guns were immaculately clean. They looked new, and the truth is, they were; none had ever been fired.

Freddy kept the shells and cartridges in a small drawer at the bottom of the gun cabinet. There was one box of shells for each gun, four boxes, four different kinds of shells. And each box was full, but the boxes were tattered and worn from years of having the cartridges taken out and handled and put back again.

Freddy and I went hunting together only once. It was a Saturday, and we drove an hour and a half to Joe Paluchek's place in Ashtabula. Paluchek worked at the plant with Uncle Freddy, but he had moved away from the east side, had gotten out, had bought ten acres in the country, or what went for country on the edges of Cleveland. Paluchek was the envy of his friends. He had a crummy house on a crummy ten acres, but it was land and it was his. I'd heard about him for years. He was the guy who could piss off his back porch, go hunting in his own back yard. An hour and a half drive from home to work, one way, was not too much to pay, and everybody knew it.

Joe came out to greet us. He was standing very straight and his chest, it seemed to me, was puffed out. He took Uncle Freddy by the hand, slapped him on the back and said, "Welcome to the country!" And Uncle Freddy looked around and said, all the way into the kitchen, "You sure got a nice place here, Joe." And Joe said, "Well, it ain't much, but it's mine and it's home and I can piss off my back porch and hunt in my own back yard." And Freddy smiled and shook his head slightly.

We sat at the kitchen table and had coffee and doughnuts and the two men talked and I listened. They did not talk about the union or the plant. They talked about hunting and game and their guns and about a fishing trip they thought they should take next summer. Finally Joe thought it was time to get going, so we put on our hunting clothes; the two men loaded their shotguns—I didn't have a gun—and we struck off into the field behind the house.

It was a hot November day and dusty. After what seemed like a very short time, Joe kicked up a cottontail and killed it, almost blowing it in half. Joe said it was a good sign, that the game was on the move today, but we thrashed through that little field the rest of the morning and never saw another living thing.

Joe's property line at the back was a chain-link fence, and beyond the fence there was a graveyard of sorts for old tractor-trailer rigs, a couple of acres probably, paved over with cement that was now heaved and cracked with age, where dozens of old tractors and trailers stood, rusting and dented, with flat tires or no tires at all and broken windshields and some broken beer bottles, and all this was silent and still, except maybe in a slight breeze the back door to one of the trailer rigs would creak slightly on its rusting hinges.

I stood for a long time, the others having gone on, with my fingers hooked into the fence and stared at the place beyond, the clutter and rubble. I turned away and moved through the grimy, little field toward the men.

It was almost dark when we got back to Alhambra Street. Joe had given us the rabbit, and we had laid it out gently on some newspaper in the trunk. By the time Uncle Freddy had parked the car in the driveway and opened the trunk, a half dozen neighbors were standing around waiting to see what we had to show. Everyone was strangely quiet, almost reverential, as they stared down on the blood soaked fur of the cottontail.

A rabbit, a wild rabbit, here, on Alhambra Street, in Cleveland, Ohio, an animal that just this morning had lived in a field, slept under a bush, drunk from a brook, an animal that lived far away, in the country, in Ashtabula. For a moment these workers in factories had been drawn away into a common past, to a time when they were all hunters, all close to the country, and their reverential silence was for that time long ago and for the sense of loss they all felt at being who and where they were now.

We gutted and skinned the rabbit, took it upstairs to the kitchen, quartered it, put it to soak, and went into the den, where we cleaned the gun, even though it had not been fired, and put it back in the gun cabinet and locked the door.

Turn left again and face the fourth and final wall. On the right is the door into this world. Attached to the rest of the wall is a long workbench. There is a grindstone and a vise bolted to it and resting on it an ashtray, two hunting knives and some fishing tackle. There is a swivel chair on casters, the kind secretaries use or people who do delicate piece-work on assembly lines.

Above the workbench is the focus of the entire room. A painting, a reproduction of an oil, big, four foot by two, on cardboard with those squiggly lines to make it look like brush strokes, of the Rockies or maybe the Tetons, with half their height above treeline and snow on the top, even now in early fall, and in the foreground a mountain meadow with flowers, asters maybe, blue anyway, and in the middleground a glacial lake, a reflecting mirror for the mountains, and on the lake, resting like a dragonfly or an aspen leaf, a canoe with a man in it fishing, alone, alone in this vast and pristine wilderness.

There are two spotlights attached to the ceiling that shine down on the painting so that Uncle Freddy can sit in the swivel chair in the dark, except for the spotlights, and be lost.

I can see him, my Uncle Freddy, sitting in his swivel chair, in the dark, spotlights on the picture, his rifle or shotgun in his hands. I can see him turn in the chair, quickly, snap the gun to his shoulder, and "Pow!" he says, "Pow!"

Again and again, night after night, year after year, I see him turning in his chair. Or fishing on that lake, his fly line unfurling, slowly, as in a dream, gracefully curving, laying out, settling softly, lightly on the skin of water.

I seem him in the double house on Alhambra Street, in his den, trapped forever, condemned to work a lathe at Picker X-ray, to spend his nights turning in that chair, around and around in his dream on Alhambra Street, turning, turning forever, my Uncle Freddy, and I hear him saying, "Pow!"

He says, "Pow!"

NORTH

North
to ancient rounded mountains—all ledge and rock outcropping,
yet softened green by forest.
Maple, beech, birch, ash and poplar. Larch, spruce, hemlock,
    cedar, pine
and fir—pointing toward the sky.

This particular place: thirty-six square miles.
A billion, billion souls, six-hundred human souls,
two-thirds in the mountains, two-hundred in the village.

One village of the many—call it Judevine.
Squeezed between sharp-rising hills, room only for
the highway, railroad, river,
and what houses could be put amongst the three.

And I, out of the city and into this place,
into these surrounding hills, into a dream
of wilderness and freedom and bread,
a dream of life growing in a solitude
where inward and outward, other and self, disappear
and the spirit of wholeness rises
definite and sweet
as dawn.

ON BEING NATIVE

The Vermont Jewish mother says:
So who's native? Don't talk to me native.

Because you got here early makes you more?

Witch grass, zucchini, tomatoes, you and me—
all immigrants is what I'm talking.
Native is dirt and stones, mountains,
What else?

We, love, are water
Oi!
Just passing through.

ANTOINE AND I GO FISHING

Saints and me! Ah quit!

Look at what we live with: Bert
and he sayin' someday he iss gonna ketch me workin'
when he come out here in da puckerbrush in his bathrom slipers
and peek araound to spy on us. Wall, someday he might be,
but, by the Jesus Christ, David, let's don't let it be today!

You know—you pra'bly don't—we been werkin'
in this lot all summer and up this loggin' road
less'n half a mile is a pond what's full a trout,
I mean, Mister, full. I been thinkin' on it all this summer
an' today's the day we go up dere an' get our supper.

Poachin' and jackin' ain't too much for me;
Ah don't go sugarin' da way ole Elwin used to
with a tank in back da trunk and gather after dark
roadside buckets offin saumbody else's trees.
That's narrah. Makin' sugar is too much work
fer dat!

But these trout here now just up da hill
is a differ'nt matter 'tirely since all Doc done
was drop a few into dat place when he built da t'ing.
Da fishes did the rest. So da way I see it
they ain't no more his 'an anybody else's since da ones
he bought be caught or died long time ago
an' what's left is only fishes what belong each odder
or demselves or to dem what hooks 'em
like da likes a you an' me.

Now how dat be? You t'ink ah cipher good enough
to get us up there?

Oh, you don't have to worry none 'bout him caumin'.
Ah know Doc, know 'im well; he'd shoot us
just like he do his gramma. Nice fella, him.

Comeon, David, ah bring you pole, put two in da trunk
this mornin'. You scratch araound, get some worm,
ah get da 'quip'ment an we go.

I did as I was told and we were gone
up the hill into the shade of trees
and to the pond. In fifteen minutes
we had half a dozen of the nicest brook trout
I have ever seen.

Then Antoine startled.
Oh! Hear that! Come on!
It's him, or Bert.
One shoot and d'odder fire.

Six trout flapping from an alder stick.
Two men run and stumble, giggle,
through the woods
back to the car.

Antoine hid the poles and fish inside his trunk
and we listened to a log truck
grinding down the hill toward the village.

Wall, six be da poacher's limit anyway.

RAYMOND KILLS A DEER

Halfway through November.
Toward evening and raining.
At the meadow's edge

low
brown
sudden

hawk. Hunter. She
who is terror to those who shudder against the earth
moves in silence

through the gray rain.
Feather soft she moves,
cold and soft,

her talons hung beneath her
limp
as broken fingers.

That night the first snow falls and whispers against the windows:
Raymond. Raymond!
Come out of your house and hunt again.

He twitches in his sleep,
in his dream he sees
a bloody carcass steam and drip.

Out in morning dark he pushes through the new snow
watching the ground,
picks up a track and follows, then

strikes off tangentially, slides across the sidehill
and circles broadly away from
what he thinks is the buck's intention,

settles under a hemlock
on a ridge of maple, ash and beech
and waits, shivers, in the dawn.

Below him, a brown spot behind gray trees.
Raymond watches down blued steel.
The buck takes a step, waits.

His eyes scan the hill,
only his ears up, pricked forward,
move.

The shot resounds three miles across the valley
strikes a ridge, returns. The deer goes down,
then rises and is gone.

He slants down the sidehill on three legs
drawing a red line
behind himself.

Seven o'clock.
Raymond will watch the drip
of this life,

follow this
unravelling thread
all day.

Off the hardwood ridge, through cedars and swamp,
over a softwood knoll, across a brook and on,
never faster than he has to, keeping just ahead

of his assassin, the murdered beast flees and bleeds
on fallen logs and withered ferns, dragging
his shattered leg through the new snow.

Across a pasture, into the sugarbush, through a sag,
down a logging road
and on.

Here, at the brook where the buck drank,
Raymond dips down, drinks too, and rests;
eats his lunch. His sandwich tastes like blood.

Later, further on, where the buck rested,
the red, red, bright-red snow
packed from his ragged shoulder.

He who is dead
is dying.
Yet he goes on.

Now Raymond sees him just ahead bounding into thick spruce.
More blood now
waist high on branches, more and more.

Then, under a wind-felled naked maple,
finally,
the killer and the killed.

Raymond pulls the hammer back and finishes
what he began
nine hours earlier.

The buck shivers;
his mouth foams blood;
his eyes bleed.

Twitch, twitch.
Twitch.
Twitch.

Quick
and simple
as that.

Raymond sits at the murdered head,
strokes the murdered neck
speaks softly words of comfort.

He rolls his sleeves.
Knife in at the sternum
slices to the anus.

He dumps the steaming stomach and intestines on the ground,
cuts away the diaphram, extracts the lungs, the broken heart,
puts the liver in a bag.

Where life was,
a hole gapes.
Fat shimmers white in blood and bile.

Off the ridge now, in the dark, he comes,
bloody to the shoulders, dragging,
200 pounds of deer.

Red-faced, sweating
he moves through the cold
and starless night.

From where the rear hoof scrapes the woodshed floor to antler tip,
eight feet, this creature stretches,
hung.

Raymond leans against the woodshed door and wonders for a
moment
why he took this life.
He knows the gutless carcass does not die,

knows this winter it will rise again and run
down long red alleys through another misty wilderness
around his bloody heart.

But what his mind can comprehend is not enough.
There are too many lives in this life,
too many deaths,

and no amount of thought can save him from his grief
for dying things, not even knowing
resurrection,

sure
and green
as spring.

ANTOINE ON HUNTING AND SOME SPOOKS

David, yew go hauntin'? Ah be.
Now ah got annuder mou' ta feed.
Gonna plug a gov'ment beef.
Don't care it if be a skipper neider.
Ah ain't haunt dem har'wood ra'bits
since ah was a boy, since dat time one fall
those downcountry killers stay tu aour place.
T'ree of 'em, all aout back tagether in a baunch
see a big ol' bauck, all fire tu once,
fill dat poor ol' basserd up,
but he keep on goin', jomp over da fence,
hang all his gut out on da wire
but keep on goin'. Poor ol' basserd.
Whan ah see dat, ah quit. Dunno why.
Now ah gonna go again.

Ah haf a version a dat deer that night,
see him in mah dream jes like a spook.
He keep on raunin', den he turn araoun'
an' raun right tru dem basserds
an' keep on goin'.
Ah still see 'im all these year af'er
an' he still goin'.

Dat make me t'ink abaout are haunted house.
When ah be a pup we caum daown fraum Derby
move tew are place.

Da ol' spooks don' like da way we put da furnitur'.
We lay in bed a' night an' hear 'em daown da stairs
movin' da furnitur' 'raound da way dey like it.
We have da priest caum over bless da house;
he say spooks is friendly
all dey wan' is for da furnitur'
to be da way dey like it.
So we let 'em put it where dey wan'
an' ever't'ing be okay. Julluk 'at.

On'y ol' Babe Williams never caum intew da house.
He work daown tew da cemet'ry tew many years.
He wear 'is 'at ta bed to keep da spooks out.
He caum over tu are place
haf'ta give 'im supper on da porch.
Won't caum in.

Now ol' Babe is dead 'n' gone
just like dat bauk
an now ah see 'em bot' tagether in mah dreams.

Just las' night ah seen 'em raunnin' side by side
up da road. See right tru 'em bot'.
Ya'd t'ink dat be a scary dream
but it wan't.
Ah like to see 'em raunning der tagether.
An' dey was talkin' to each odder
while dey ran.

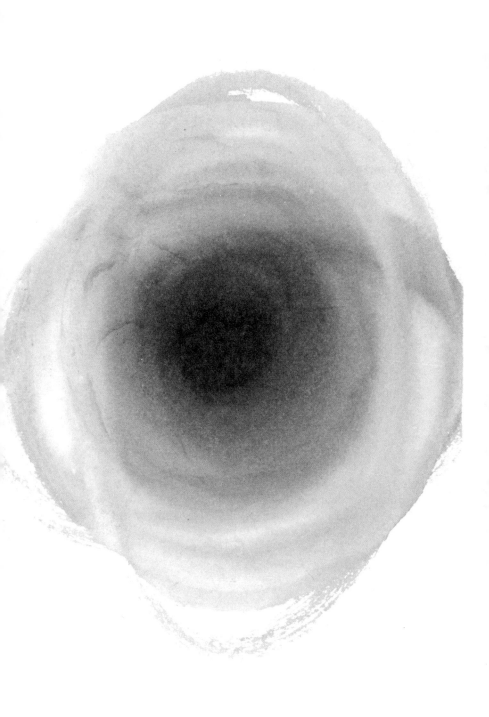

GRACE

Grace lives in a trailer on the edge of town,
down along the river. She's got three kids.
She had a husband, but he split.
I saw a questionaire once that she'd filled out
asking if they'd volunteer at school.
Here is what she said.

> I'd like to but I got no time.
> We get up at half past five, my husband and myself I
>   mean
> and he is out the door by 6:15.
> Then I get up the kids and them and me all leave
> together a little after seven.
> I take Doreen to school, then drop the other two
> at Mrs. Fairchild's and then I go to work myself.
> When I get done I pick up the kids to Fairchild's
> and we get home by six.
> My husband, he gets home about an hour later.
> By the time we get our supper there's no time left
>   for nothin'.
> We live like this six days a week, even Saturdays,
> and Sundays, we try to work around the place,
> you know,
> get in the wood or fix the goddamned car.

Since her husband left she's given up her full-time job
and things for Grace and for the kids have gone down hill
which is no doubt one of the reasons she got into so much trouble . . .
but, ah . . . Grace will speak for herself.

> The hell I will.

Well, she can speak for herself.

> You're goddamned right I can.

Will you? Please.

I got nothin' to say.

You do too.

Why do you want me to do this anyway?

It's your chance to have your say, to tel your side
and tell it like you want it told.

Why should I bother?
Nobody listens anyway.

I will.

Big fuckin' deal.

Thanks. Are you going to tell your story?

Alright.
Alright, Mr. Poet, only
maybe you won't like it.

Maybe.

I suppose you want to hear about the time I had to
go to court.

That'd be a good place to start.

Voyeur, ain't ya?

Yes. Just like everybody else.

True enough.
Only everybody else don't write it down.
Where the hell do you get off, anyway?
Write this down, you bastard.
You're a son-of-a-bitch, is what I think.
Who in hell do you think you are undressing all of us
in public?

. I've heard about those poems you write. I've heard
that's what you do. Oh, I know how you do it, sure,
you just rearrange things, just enough so none of us
can sue. I know how you do it. Fiction. Fiction, shit.
I can barely read but I know fiction.
Those stupid assholes read your stuff, they really think
you made us up?

I made up you!

    Bullshit to that. How could you?
    I'm talkin' to you ain't I?
    Christ you're stupider that I thought!

Are you gonna tell your story, Grace, or are you gonna dump
    on me?

    Maybe I'll do both.

Fine!

    You just want me to embarrass myself don't you?

No! I just want you to have your chance!

    Alright. Alright. But nobody will listen.
    Nobody around here ever listens. Everybody around
        here . . .

You already said that.

    Shut up! I'm talkin' ain't I?
    Everybody around here already knows what they think
        of me.
    They think I'm a beast or something, think
    I'm not sorry for that time. Well, maybe I'm not.
    How about that? Maybe I'm not sorry.

    I didn't mean to hurt her. She's my baby, ain't she?
    For Christ's sake, she came out of me.
    All I wanted was some quiet. What's so wrong with that?

She was screaming, I mean screaming.
She'd been doing it for days. You can only stand so
    much of that you know.
I stood as much as I could stand and then I hit her.
I hit her and I hit her and I hit her. I wanted to . . .
I . . .

Do you understand? No. No. You don't. Because you
    can't.
Because you are always in control, you always got
    yourself together.
You couldn't understand. You could never understand.

I love my baby more than you or anybody will ever
    know.
I love her and I wanted to break her face.
Both. Both. Both those things! Not just one.
Goddamnit, not just one.

That's what I told the judge, but he's just like you.

Anymore on that?

    No.

What about the way they say you sleep around?

    Gimme a break will you?
    Who says that, Edith? Christ.

    How could I? When? David, do you know what my life
        is like?
    I would if I could, if I ever got the chance.
    Why not?
    You think I'm made of stone or somethin'? You think
    I wouldn't like to have somebody I could be with,
    share all my troubles with, do chores and keep this place
    together with? You think I wouldn't like that?
    To have somebody to sleep up next to, to hold on to?
    To fuck? . . .

You're goddamned right, Mister, because it's comfort.
It's warm and good, I mean, sometimes it can be.
Fun. Fun is what I mean. Some fun.

We could stay home all day some day in the middle of
    the week,
just him and me, and lounge around all morning,
have lunch together, take a bath and get in bed
and make love and stay in bed together, naked,
and watch TV all afternoon
until the kids come home from school.

You don't think I'd like that?
By Jesus, you are a fool.

You and everybody else in this goddamned place.
I hate this place! I hate it. And I hate you.

I'd get out of here tomorrow if I could.

I'd go someplace if there was someplace I could go.

I'd take the kids and go. I mean it.
I don't care what people say, to hell with them,
and you, and this goddamned place too.

Vermont! Vermont. Fuck Vermont.
And fuck you too.
I'm not sayin' any more.

TOMMY STAMES

Tommy Stames spent 18 months in Vietnam. Pleiku, Hue.
Names, strange, not at all like Judevine.
He was a hero when he got home.
Folds around here were proud of him, or if they weren't
they didn't say so. He had done his duty
and that was that.
Don't doubt it. It is true.
Everybody tried to make him feel at home
in his home. Some said he was nervous;
he had changed. Or maybe it was they
who moved around him circling at a distance
like dogs around a bear, wondering
what it was was in their midst.

When deer season came, Tom got his deer,
as he had always done, every year, since he was twelve.
He was the greatest hunter on the hill
and now everybody knew he was somehow even greater.
One shot dropped his buck, as always, and,
as always, as the seven times before,
he dressed his deer in the accustomed way,
opening the belly from sternum to vent,
his knife slipping cleanly through the hide and flesh.
Then a new maneuver.

His knife rung the genitals, extracting penis
and the testicles and with them a tab of belly skin.
He hung them by the fleshy ribbon in a tree
just as he had done
in Vietnam.

When the people heard of it, the men snickered and said
they'd have to try that next year
and the circle widened and we moved at a distance,
like dogs around a bear, wondering,
what it was was in our midst.

GOSSIP AT THE RINK

The organ stops and the skaters glide off the floor
and those there from Judevine are drawn toward each other
by some kind of communal bond, a friendship, in the presence of
so many other strangers—except, that is, Grace and Tommy
who have also come here this afternoon but now keep a distance
from the others. As Bobbie and Doug undo their skates
Conrad wobbles up to them.

Way to go, Dougie, way to go. I want to tell ya,
you skate good.

    You ain't so bad yourself, Conrad.

Well, thing is, I can skate, but I can't twirl.like you can.
You're good at twirlin', Doug.

    You should practice.

Well, I dunno about that. Ho! Speakin' a twirls,
here comes Edith. Hi, Edith, how you doin'?

    No better. I guess you could see how Grace
    was hangin' all over that Tommy Stames here
    this afternoon.

I'm kinda glad to see them two together.

    I think it's terrible.

God, you think everything is terrible, Edith.

    You can make all the fun you want, Doug . . .

Why, thank you, Edith, I think I will.

    but I heard they're shackin' up together.

I know they are, Edith.

They been livin' together about a month now, Edith.
By the Jesus, Conrad, Edith here is slippin',
She ain't keepin' her ear tight enough to the ground!

I know it! Hey, Edith, you got to keep that thing pressed tight
if you're gonna keep up with the news!

Go ahead you two, but you'd think she'd have
a little shame or modesty or something
after that awful trial and . . .

It was a hearin', Edith, not a trial; it was a hearin'
and it was a long time ago.

Well, I think the two of them hitchin' up together
is gonna be nothin' but trouble.

Why is that, Edith?

You know very well why, Conrad. You heard
what he did with that deer up in the woods.
Vietnam did something to that boy.

Vietnam did something to us all.

What'd he do, Edith? What'd he do? I want to hear
you say it. What'd he do?

Hold on, Edith, hold on. You're not a hunter.
You don't know what goes on up in the woods. You just leave . . .
you leave the woods right out of it. You don't . . . you don't
know.

It's no use with the two of you.
There are children involved here.
I'm thinking about the children.

Gawd!

You're thinking about yourself, Edith, like you always do.

That boy is a potential madman.

Why he's not!

    He's a stick of dynamite
    ready to go off in somebody's face.

    He's a good man.

Calm yourself, Edith, calm yourself! You're off the handle!
I see Tommy with them kids and he treats 'em good. He loves
them kids just like he does Grace. You can tell.

    There are lives at stake here, children's lives!
    Why, you know what they do. They lie around all day
    up in that trailer naked and drink beer and smoke dope!

    Yeow! It sounds like heaven to me!

    You know they're doin' that.

    Conrad, they're doin' that!

They're doin' what?

    They're doin' that!

They're doin' that?

    Oh, my God, they're doin' that!

I wish to hell I was doin' that. It beats roller skatin'!

I am thinking of this community.
I am just standing up for what is right!

Oh, sure, sure you are. And you're an authority
on what's right, too, aren't ya, Edith? Why, of course you are.
Why . . . you watch that Bill Donahue show!

Edith, why don't you leave them two alone?
Probably they got troubles of their own.
Why don't you do somethin' else with all your extra time.
Why don't ya learn to skate. Learn ta skate, Edith.
Save us all and learn to skate.

Bobbie, I'm surprised at you. Why don't you speak up?
This is a terrible thing that is happening here.

Come on, Bobbie, let's go home.

Snip, snip, snip, all the time, Edith. Fer God's sake!
Snip, snip, snip. Come on, Bobbie, let's go home.
Snip, snip, snip. Jesus Christ, Edith. Snip, snip, snip.

Bobbie, Doug and Conrad abandon Edith, leaving her alone.

Out in the parking lot, in Tommy's car, Tommy and Grace sit
drinking beer and Southern Comfort, when Tommy says,

I . . . ah . . . I made a little poem for you.

You did?

Ah . . . yeah . . . you want to hear it?

Sure.

A FLEETING ANIMAL

When you abandon everything
    and give yourself to me
when I abandon everything
    and give myself to you
we make a fleeting animal

of such beauty, passion,
    nakedness and grace
that I am glad it slips away
    when we are done
because this world is hurt
    and cruel and nothing
that naive and loving
    and unashamed
could possibly survive.

ANTOINE ON THE BOWSER FACTORY,
FREE ENTERPRISE, WOMEN, LOVE
AND LONELINESS

November and a foot of snow.
We've been skidding trees all day through the wet and cold.
The working day is over, everyone is gone
but Antoine and myself and Antoine still talking
as he has been all afternoon
as we sit in the cluttered truck changing rubber boots
for leather ones.

Ah, David, ah'm gettin' sick of dis.
Ah can't stand it too much longer.
We got to open dat bowser factoree like we talk about.
Make dem pussy wigs for da wimens.
Red one, yellow one, black kinky one,
red-white-an'-blue one for da pa'tri'its . . .
Dat be da t'ing!

In dis country, David, yew can't get ahead workin' out like dis.
Yew got to go it on yer own, haf saum 'magination,
be da boss, not just another sla'f like we be here day af'er day.
Yew and me, David, put are money all tagether open up dat
    factoree.
We go 'raound fraum door to door, sell dem wigs,
tell da wimens, "Hey, it be da latest t'ing."
And we be da fidders, yew and me!
Saum job!

First place we go
be to dat hippy girl what live up da road from our place.
Why,
she be saumt'ing like you never see!

Saints in da trees! What we do widout da wimens!
Dis life ain't built for to live it all alone.
Ah be forty-five, dat half of ninety, what ah'll never see,
before ah find my wimens. An' all dem years ah livin' to myself
in dat tin can with nauthin' but my goddamn dawg.
We ain't built for to live dat way.
You got to have somebody be wit', saumbody talk to, cry wid',

roll around da bed, sid across the table from.
You can't live touchin' nauthin' but a goddamn dawg.

Da Lord make plenty mistake when he build this place an' us
is what ah t'ink, on'y yew don't ell da pries' ah say so.
But one t'ing he got right was when he made da wimens.
David, yew know what I mean—how yer han' ache to hold 'er.
Dey be so different fraum da likes a hus.
Like mah cat an' dawg what loves each odder an' don't fight
only cuddle up and lick each odder all da time.

Wimens is good for da pecker an' da soul,
and, Mister, you get 'em both'n one like I got
an' like dat Raymond used ta have, an' I mean,
you got saumthin' better than da world!

Aow! All dis takin' make me itch to see her,
haf' saum tea an' touch'er face.
So why ah be here wid you all da afternoon?
Goodbye. Ah see you!

And he drove away, a cigaret
dangling from the corner of his mouth,
his arm out the window waving.

HOMAGE TO THOMAS HARDY

(after his poem "The Harbour Bridge")

An early morning drive down off the hill
To go somewhere or get something in Morrisville.
The what or where I can't remember now.
This happened years ago. What stays is how,
Curving side by side, the river and the road
Turned quickly pink and how the valley glowed,
And how dark pines and fir tuned briefly yellow-green
    in a light sudden and serene.

And how as I lounged slowly down the river road
The other cars sped 'round and by, load after load
of commuters off the hills toward work as far
Away as Burlington, racing in their cars
Toward jobs in gas stations, factories, banks and mines,
Toward schools, construction sites, shops of every kind;
Hurrying, sleepy-eyed, they passed as in a dream
    in a light sudden and serene.

Then, I saw, parked in a turn-off on my right,
A car, dirty and old, facing the brilliant light;
It's windshield broad and slightly silver-green
As if it were the Bijou's movie screen,
And on the screen I briefly saw a man,
Red-faced, behind the wheel who shook his hand
At a crying woman slouched against the door, demeaned
    in a light sudden and serene.

As I came toward them I thought I saw him say,
"You whore . . . You!" He made a fist. "You'd lay . . . "
He struck her face. "Oh, shit! Goddam you, I . . . "
Gone. Their car growing smaller in my mirror, my
mind's eye. To this day for me they remain
Frozen, the film broken, a photograph of hate and pain,
Two players, beside the road on a movie screen
    in a light sudden and serene.

WHAT I HEARD AT ROY McINNES'

I was down to Roy McInnes' welding shop one January day
when Guy Desjardins, trucker of logs and lumber,
pulled his log truck in.

Guy hopped down out of the cab and immediately began
that little wintertime dance we all do where you
exhale rapidly and hop back and forth from foot to foot
while you pat your hands and say,
"Jesus! Roy, is it cold enough for you?"

I can't remember what Roy said to that
but you are supposed to think something funny.

Guy said "Hi" to me and I said "Hi" to him and the three of
    us
gathered around Roy's quadruple-chamber oil-drum stove.

They began to talk and I began to listen.

    Where you workin' now, Guy?

        I'm drawing logs and pulp off the landing
        up to where Antoine and Doug are cuttin',
        the old Mead place, on the other side of Bear Swamp.
        You know the place?

    Well I guess I do.
    My grandmother lived up there when she was just a little girl
    before my family came down off the mountain
    and settled down here in the village and got civilized.

        They did, did they? How come it never took with you?

    I've wondered that myself.
    Speakin' of wild ones, is that Stames boy
    still workin' with those loonies?

        Yes sir, he still is.
        He's been workin' with them steady
        since early this past fall.

    Huh. He's stuck with them that long. Huh.

Yes sir.

It may be that that boy is settlin' down.

    Well, you know. He's got himself a little family now.
    What with Grace and the kids and all that kind of thing.
    I think it gives him something to look forward to,
    something to go to work for,
    and Jesus Christ, you know
    a woman's good for any man.

No. I didn't know.

TOMMY AGAIN FINALLY ·

Antoine and Doug and Tommy cut logs and pulp right through
    that winter and into spring.
When the black flies came out they gave up working in the woods
and each went his separate way, found summer jobs, or no jobs
    at all.

Tommy went on living with Grace and they both seemed happy
    as far as anybody could tell
and Grace's kids did too.

I saw Grace down to Jerry's once that next spring and she had
    a pretty bad shiner,
but nobody said anything about it, and what people thought,
if anything, I can't say.

Then it was summer, the middle of July . . .

Tommy Stames shot himself.

    What? What? What'd you say?

Tommy Stames killed himself.

    What'd you say?

He shot himself up to his camp.

    Where? Up to his camp?

Up to his camp. Antoine came and got me.

    Tommy Stames killed himself. He shot himself.

Where?

    He killed himself. Up to his camp.

Antoine came and got me. He left Antoine a note.
All it said was: *Thank you, Antoine.*
You know where to find me.

He shot himself?

Antoine came and got me. We went up.
We . . . We brought him back. He knew.

Tommy killed himself. He killed himself.

Tommy went up to his favorite place,
that little clearing in the woods.

He had a little camp up there, a fireplace,
a little lean-to made of spruce poles and
hemlock boughs.
Why, he camped up there.

And in the lean-to
there was a book of ancient Chinese poetry

and a Chinese painting
one of those long skinny ones
that start down close
and go up way up far
up into the mountains

and way up in the mountains in that painting
there was a little place

the Chinese called them pavilions
but it was just a lean-to

˙ and a man sitting out in front of it,
just a tiny spot,
all alone
way up in the mountains.

Just like Tommy's place
and just like Tommy.

You go up through the woods and you cross a little stream
and you come to this clearing in the forest
where the light comes in.

Before he killed himself
he made a circle out of stones he'd gathered from the stream
and in the circle there were bits of bark and twigs,
little signs or symbols,
something.

You go up through the woods and cross a little stream.

Antoine came and got me. We went up. We brought him back.

A clearing in the forest where the light comes in.

He camped up there.
It was a little lean-to in the forest.

He put himself in the middle of that circle.
He was sitting down.
He took his army carbine . . .

You go up through the woods.

He left a note for Antoine.

You cross a little stream.

A clearing in the forest.

And he shot himself right through the heart.
He knew exactly where his heart was at.
He didn't miss.

He fell backward on the ground. He was laid out on the ground.

Like Jesus on the cross,

with his arms spread out.

He died right away and right inside that stone circle
he had made with the pebbles from the stream.

You could tell he didn't suffer.
He looked so peaceful, like he felt good . . .
like he finally felt good.

In the forest where the light comes in.

And on his shirt he had pinned
a little piece of paper
and on it he had written:

Grace and Peace be with Me.

HOW I CAME TO GET THE POEMS
THAT TOMMY WROTE FOR GRACE

It was the fall after Tommy died.
The phone rang one morning and it was Grace.
She said she had something she wanted to show me, to give me,
could she come up. I said sure and she hung up.

I was shocked and curious and anxious and excited
by her forwardness, her reaching out to me. It wasn't like her
or anyone else in these parts. I waited by the window
watching for her car. Then I saw it down on the road
slowing to make the turn into the drive and up to the house.
She got out of the car, reached back in to get a large, Manila,
clasp-type evelope, closed the door, turned
and moved up the sloping lawn toward the house cradling the
    envelope in her arms and pressing it against her breasts
    the way school girls carry their books.
I was waiting on the porch.
She looked directly at me, smiled and said, "Hi."

I said "Hi" and something about the clarity and warmth and color
of the day and Grace nodded as if to tell me
she didn't want to go through all that bullshit socializing.

    I'm sorry to bother you.
    I could have sent you these,
    but I wanted to hand them to you face to face.
    It's not easy.
    I know we've had our differences, but I . . .

I broke in and said that I was pleased and glad and flattered
that she'd come to see me and then, although I began to
    stumble,
I started saying how I knew how hard it was to reach out and
how hard it must be for her right now.

    For shit's sake, David, can it.
    You talk too goddamned much.
    I don't need your help,
    and I don't want your explanations either.
    I came up here to give you these
    and to tell you why I wanted to.
    Just give me a chance,
    will you please?

47

I'm sorry.
But I said it wasn't easy.

Grace cast down her eyes.
An awkward silence stood between us.

Would you like some coffee?

She raised her head and looked at me again.
In her eyes there was an intensity of stare,
a depth of rage and pain and a warm affection
that made me shudder.

Yes. That would be nice. Thank you.

I went inside to fix the coffee and left Grace sitting in
      a lawn chair on the porch.
I came back with a pot of coffee on a tray, two mugs,
two spoons, sugar, half and half and a few pieces
of anisette toast on a small plate. I set it down
on the overturned wooden box we used for a coffee table
and poured.

This is nice. Thank you.

She smiled at me again, then fixed her coffee and settled back into
her chair.

I know we've had our differences
and in lots of ways I still think
you are a royal asshole,
but being a poet and all, well,
I thought maybe you would understand,
besides, I mean,
who else could I turn to?

No offense intended, but
you're the best that I can do.

Shit, I always do that.
I always say the wrong thing.
Aw, what the hell. It's the way I am.

What's in that envelope is Tommy's poems,
I mean the ones he wrote for me.
I wanted to share them.
I wanted to show them to somebody.

Huh. Probably now you too will think
what Edith and everybody else around here says
is true, probably you'll think I'm pretty kinky,
being as, you'll see, they are mostly pretty sexy.

But I thought I'd bring them to you anyway.
I mean, I think they're good.
And I thought maybe someday
you could put them in a book.

SOME OF THE POEMS THAT TOMMY WROTE FOR GRACE

THANK YOU

Life is short
and every day
I am so afraid.
Every day
I know such anguish,
such
sorrow, sadness, pain.
Every day
I am so afraid.

Thank you, woman,
for being here with me,
for sleeping next to me,
for looking at me naked,
for touching me,
for putting your mouth on me.

You are comfort,
you are peace,
you are love and warmth
for me.

LOVER, STRANGER, FRIEND

How can it be?
Just a year ago
I didn't even know
your name, I
had never seen
your face.

What or who
let us know each other
in this way?
What or who
has blessed us,
given us
this peace?

Lover, stranger, friend,
this nakedness I have with you—
it is a balm, a gift
to soothe
my wounded life,
my loneliness.

THESE HANDS

These fingertips,
these flattened palms,
the way these hands
can make a cup
to touch you,
touch you.

Oh.

These hands
with which
to hold you.

SOMA

There is this
soft and furry thing
between your thighs

that I
touch with fingers
kiss with lips

come into and
lose myself within.

There is this soft
and furry thing,

rank and wet
and dark and rich

that takes me in
and says to me,

come into me,
forget
your sorrow and depression,
give up
your pain and agony.

Come into me.
Let all your sadness go.
Lose yourself in me.

PLEA

I am dying. I don't want to die.
I want to stay like this forever.
The two of us coupled, joined together.

We are alive and breathing.
I can hear us.
I can feel us.

We are joined together.
We are alive and breathing.

I am dying. I don't want to die.

THE ANGEL OF DEPRESSION

The angel of depression
came today
and took my soul away.
She left my body
lying on this bed
curled in upon itself as if
I had not yet
been born.

The angel of depression
came today
and left me motionless,
lying still as death,
waiting here

until her brighter sister,
the one who looks like you,
comes to take me in her arms
and raise me up
and put her mouth on mine
and breathe back into me
my life.

SOME QUESTIONS FOR THE ANGEL OF DEPRESSION

When you
take my soul from me

where do you go with it
and what do you do
and why do you take it anyway
and how come I can't
protect myself from you
and why
once you've taken it
why
do you let your brighter sister
bring it back to me?

WAIT

I can see
the sadness of your life
today.
I can see it
in your eyes.

There is no touch
no kiss, no sigh
today
that can save you
from your pain.

You have turned within yourself
today
and wrapped yourself
around your wounded friend
the one whose name
is Anger-Grief
and who lives behind your eyes.

There is nothing I can do today
but watch you suffer,
nothing I can do but wait
for your wounded friend to leave.

I can see the sadness
of your life today.
I can see it in your eyes.

And tomorrow
I will be the one
who moves across our lives
dancing my own sorrow-dance
with my own wounded friend,

and tomorrow
will you, please,
be the one
who waits for me.

PRIESTESS

When you cup your hands
around your breasts
and hold them up
and squeeze them
and offer them to me,

I think you are
an ancient priestess
covered with oil and perfume
and I am the common, ordinary
worshipper who has come
hot and tired
out of the dusty fields
and into your temple.

When I see you coming toward me
I am terrified.
My heart is in my throat.
I can't breathe.
When I see your hands
cupped around your breasts
and you offering them to me,
I think I hear you saying:

Here, drink from these,
drown in these.
They are filled with milk.
It is warm and sweet.
Suffocate and drown
and die in these.
They will ease your pain.
They are comfort.
They are peace.

Here, drown in these.
They are warm
and they are sweet.

Here, drink from these.
It is milk.
It is warm and it is sweet.

SOMETIMES

Sometimes after I
get out of the shower
after I have dried myself
before we come together
to love each other and
if it is already hard
I will hang my towel from it
and parade around this place
telling you
that I am the world's first
walking, talking towel rack,
and sometimes
while I am doing that
I think about the meaning
of our love and I wonder
if I have the courage
to tell you what I
so much believe, which is:
My rod and my staff
will comfort you!
And it will also comfort me.

These bodies we give each other,
they will give us comfort,
they will give us peace.

Because of what we feel together,
because of what we touch and see,
we will have peace.

PRAISE FOR MY LIFE

The garden is free of weeds.
The vegetables blossom and grow large.

This woman is beautiful and gentle.
her children are loving and kind.

In the cool of the evening
the kids and the dogs

romp and clown on the lawn
and the night birds begin to sing.

What man could ever be as lucky
as I am?

NOT MUCH

Union
Oneness
Ecstasy

is all
I ever
wanted.

LAST POEM

The angel of depression came today
and this time took
both my body and my soul
away.

She told me
to leave this note for you
to tell you
that her brighter sister,
that's the one who looks like you,
will not be allowed to save me.

She says this time no one
will be allowed to save me.

The angel of depression
came today
and this time
she didn't only
take my soul away,
this time

I went with her.

REPRISE

I made a poem for you. You wanna hear it?
  Sure.
    Tommy Stames shot himself. He killed himself.

What? What did you say?
  He shot himself. He killed himself.
    Up to his camp.

You go through the woods and you cross a little stream.
  It was a clearing in the forest
    where the light comes in.

He had a little lean-to
  and a fireplace
    and a book of Chinese poetry.

And on his shirt he had pinned a little piece of paper.
  And on it he had written:
    Grace and Peace be with Me.

This never ending dream—
  You sure got a nice place here, Joe—
    of wilderness and freedom and bread.

I made a poem for you.
  I made a poem for you.
    Grace and Peace be with Me.

GRACE AGAIN

It must have been at least a year between the time
Grace came up to give me Tommy's poems and when I saw her
    next.

I had just pulled in to Jerry's, gotten out of the car and
was headed into the store, my head down thinking about
    something,
as Grace was coming out. She saw me first.

    Oh! Hi, David. Hi.

Well, I'll be . . . . Hi, Grace. Boy, it's been a long time.

    Yes, it has.

My gosh, it is nice to see you.

    It's nice to see you too.

How you doin'?

    Good. Good. Real good.

That's terrific. I'm really glad to hear that.

    I got a new boy friend now.

Good. That's terrific.

    We been goin' together, let's see, must be, hell,
    since last winter sometime anyway. I was workin'
    as a chambermaid down to Stowe, at the Edelweiss,
    you know. He always stays at the Edelweiss
    when he comes up to Stowe.

That's terrific.

    Yeah, and it's workin' out good too. He's good to me
    and good to the kids too. He always brings us presents,
    the kids and me, I mean.

He's got pots of money. I mean, David, he is rich.
Like you don't know. He runs an import business
in New York, or somethin', I don't know. I mean he
is rich! He's good to me.

He's got an apartment in the city, up on the upper east side.
83rd Street. It looks out over the East River, 34th floor,
and, I mean, big too! With big floor to ceiling windows
that look out on to the river and across to Queens
and Brooklyn. God, the Brooklyn bridge is so beautiful
at night. The Queensboro bridge is too, that's the one
right close to where we live, but not so much, not so much
as the Brooklyn bridge. I just love to stand at those
windows after the kids are all in bed and watch the river
and the lights and all the lights reflected in the river.
I never thought I'd like New York, but it is beautiful!
David, it is beautiful. Well, hell, you know that.
You lived there, didn't you?

I mean, we got it good. We go down there, the kids and me
and stay with him when the kids are out of school.
He won't let us come while the kids are doin' school.
He says they've got to get their education.
He's good to them. I mean, he really cares for them.
And he is big on education.

But when the kids are out of school, he sends his plane
right up here to Burlington. He's got a private plane
and a private pilot too. He sends his plane right up
to Burlington and we drive in and meet it. We fly down
to LaGuardia and his chauffeur and his limosine
picks us up and takes us right up to the door of his
apartment building. I mean, is that good or what?
How can you beat that?

He's also got a place down in the Caribbean.
It's a little island, he owns the whole damn thing,
off one of those bigger islands, I don't know which one.
He's got some kind of mansion, a chateau, a private beach
and everything. He says the water is so clear you can see
clear to the bottom right down through sixty feet.

I haven't been down there to that one yet, but we're all
going down come wintertime this year. He says he's getting
sick of these Vermont winters and he's also getting sick
of Stowe. Well, shit. I said yes to that! You can imagine
what I said to that!

He says to hell with skiing and to hell with Stowe.
He says we are all going to the Caribbean this winter,
about the first of December is what he said. I'm going
to take the kids out of school and we're all gong down there
for the winter. He's going to get the kids a private tutor.
He's already got a housekeeper and a cook down there. He's
really big on education. He says my kids have got to get
and education so they don't end up like me and have to spend
their whole lives working by the hour down to Stowe.
I mean, he is big on education.

Oh, Jesus! Look what time it is. I got to go.
Every afternoon about this time, he calls me on the telephone.
No matter where he is, he calls me on the telephone.
If he's in the limosine he calls me on the mobile phone.
He always wants me home to get his call. I got to go.

Jesus, David, it's been nice to see you.
How you been? You still livin' up there on the hill?
I got to go.

It's been nice to see you, David.
I wish I could talk a little longer, but
he calls me every afternon. I got to go.

Take care, David.
It's been nice to see you.

KYRIE

Have mercy upon us, oh Lord.
Lord, have mercy upon us.